Significant Wow

for sad girls

Significant Wow

Emily Cotterill

Seren is the book imprint of
Poetry Wales Press Ltd.
Suite 6, 4 Derwen Road, Bridgend,
Wales, CF31 1LH

www.serenbooks.com
Follow us on social media @SerenBooks

ISBN: 978-1-78172-772-0
ebook: 978-1-78172-774-4

A CIP record for this title is available from the British Library.

The publisher acknowledges the financial assistance of the Books Council of Wales.

Cover painting: *Spaghetti Arms* by Lucia Jones

Printed in Bembo by 4Edge Ltd, Hockley.

Contents

The Greatest Punk Album in the World Ever (Disc Two)

I am consciously, consciously
picking up women – to carry
in my pockets, to throw
at rough walls in moments
when something might make
them stick. I have lined my back
teeth with Viv Albertine,
replaced my extremities
with Patti Smith. I have built
a soft curve around a sad razor.
There is blood in my mouth
that's familiar. I do the things
men do, just better. I have swapped
my memories for a future.
but when I whimper,
hear Debbie Harry scream.

The yarn-bombers don't know

I'm at war with them. I only rip off their rain-soaked small world
kitsch in my imagination. I am as unobtrusive as they are. My edges
are softening. I fascinate myself with destruction and spray-paint
but the crocheted mice of reality still live their post-box topping lives,
tiny slices of unknowable cake, stuck on the way to undetailed mouths.
Who has the time for woollen graffiti? Who is the parish-councillor,
god of village greens and bunting? In the phone-box library, I turn
romance spines to face inward, bury novels under German readers,
and manuals for toasters long taken by landfill. I know what they don't,
that *British Telecom* is coming, with binbags and polite notices,
to take all this chaos apart. I drink three beers on the grass
of the Public Space Protection Order alcohol prohibited space.
In my sun-stroked half dreams, the mouse people twitch into reality,
swarm down to meet me, tiny faces twisted in a picture postcard of hate.

Installing a Terrarium in the Town Square

Take the children from the edge of learning. Bring them,
with their crumpled permission slips through drizzle –
to see the stopper go in. Place commemorative paving
by the discount supermarket. Seal the glass in a second layer –
so kicked pebbles won't crack the archived atmosphere.

Over the years graffiti will grow wide across the outside,
long small eclipses, throwing the name of a bored boy
into the path of photosynthesis. In the dark, the curve
of the glass will hold the S bend of a ready girl's back.

The same green plants live, die and grow. Eventually
the children from the ceremony head to comprehensive,
knowing when our dystopia comes, they were there –
at the blind hope of saving something. When they panic,
do it too, use your knuckles, break all the glass.

The Day of the Flying Ants

When did we learn that flying ants are not another species, just another sex?

I saw us twice today while the air was thick with wingbeats:
once we were children, chlorine fresh from swimming
waiting on leisure centre steps – the other teenagers,
kissing loudly with wet mouths and worried hands.

On the day the ants fly, I miss our possibilities most,
remember them crawling on our bare legs?

Somewhere new queens are making their nests
and that reminds me – I should have had you –
terrified, while your mum folded sheets on the landing.

The Bar in This Poem Has Closed

It hurts to be out but when it comes to it –
you can take an empty bottle from the next table,
grasp it by the slender stem of the neck
and smash it in the bowl of this bar's toilet.
Now you have a weapon against sadness.

Years later, when you step back into the scene
of this crime, you remember the entire wardrobe
of that night. Tell your friends you feel fine,
scratch dry skin, drink from soda taps all night.

Love Song to a Poster Boy

Even now I have peeled the last *Blu-tac* from the back
of you, my teenage heart remembers how you were
the perfect hook for grappling with. Exposed steel
while I was desperate for a grip to grow an adulthood.
Spinning flesh and sinew around ideas almost in the image
of you. Becoming a pearl, if pearls were scared and raw

and clinging. The earth shakes but you won't move – not
without an avalanche, a landslide. Not without
the stuttering collapse of this whole nervous inside.
Almost everything has changed, but when I check
my heart is still overflowing, and the look of you makes
the palm of my hand ache for the crook of your elbow.

Slag

I have loved coal,
like a teenage girl loves
an older guitarist with a rough
black smudge of eyeliner.
I have built my life on it,
screamed down decades for it,
'coal not dole' – bared my soul
for it, but old women gossip
about the pit. I know the world
has had enough of it.

Coal – with its head full
of history, strong arms,
filthy engines, heavy,
the small town sex of it.
Broken bodies, white
knuckle wives, the silence
of canaries – has risen
from slag heaps and pitheads
to thick air spluttering
into anyone born late
with an old miners' lungs.

I have loved coal but recently,
when I sit in the fresh
place built on the scar
of my grandfather's pit,
I have loved birdsong, greenspace
the safety and hope of it.
Wind turbines, rising
white beacons, sharp armed,
slicing clean paths to a future.

When My Father Dies

I will fight any man who mentions god at the funeral.
Dad believes in step-on-a crack, break-your-back
and the youthful power of the Rock of Aphrodite.
He does not hold with your organisation.
He does not hold with much.

We were at our best in that Portuguese supermarket,
when Cliff Richard signed bottles of his rosé wine
and we, more uninterested than unimpressed, browsed
around the queue for souvenirs. Let's not have stuff.

Someone else will have to make the baklava for the wake
because I will be in Cyprus, feet on warm ground,
eyes on the old coast, waiting for him to swim
back from around the nearside of his youth rock.

A Speculative Script for Motherhood

Normally the kids I don't want, are quiet.
Sometimes, I picture myself at a kitchen
island, waiting for teenage girls to fall in
from school and justify all this space.

Two members of the house are vegan.
It is always September and I am married
to an older, famously attractive actor.

But mostly, the children are quiet.
I cannot invite anyone into the world
just for that. Parts of me are getting younger,
scared of piss and tantrums and boys.

30 – 50 Feral Hogs

*'Legit question for rural Americans – How do I kill the 30-50 feral hogs that run into
my yard within 3-5 mins while my small kids play?' @WillieMcNabb, Twitter – 4/8/19*

I live in a terraced house in Manchester.
I live in a second floor flat in Sutton on Sea.
The hogs are finding their way into my living
room. They scuttle up the drainpipe, tear
through the smallness of my unclean kitchen.

They pour out of my phone's tinny speaker.
I cannot open my cupboards for fear of the hogs
escaping. They are trapped between the pages of
my cookery books. I can only take so many hogs
by the tusks at once – turn their heads as they

manoeuvre themselves to the softest parts of
my flesh. I cannot expose my back for a moment.
The hogs are everywhere once your eyes are open
and the sounds of their hooves are coming.

To Be Mindful (Type A+)

Consider the unthreatening men of blood donation,
bobbing 'round community centres and sports halls
on any given Tuesday. They dish out *Club* orange biscuits
and cheap squash in flimsy plastic cups, getting on
with institutional good. Notice machines that beep,
beep, pleasingly, cradles that rock with dark bags
of warm generous plasma. Feel the slow pressure-pull
of extraction against exposed skin on soft forearms.
See someone's postman pricking their finger on the point
of an iron test. Look, a foam javelin has come loose
from the rafters, is sinking. Look, you are slumped
on the reclining couch, sugar-weak. And safe arms,
wrapped in well-worn uniform are rushing out to catch.

John King (Disambiguation)

A pirate, clutches of politicians, and an Irish hurler,
there are 73 John Kings listed on *Wikipedia*.
But not one is the one with the name that I know –
pinned to a Derbyshire infant school and a small museum
on the slope to the wharf of his homeland (open on Sundays
in the car park, up against the bottle bank.)

Inventor of the mine cage detaching hook is not exactly
glamorous but then, what is glamorous compared to catching
and catching and catching our gene pools? Our same
shared history. Lifelines. The stuff that gave me
the same face as my father or elsewhere
that specific dark-eyed valleys beauty.

All those bodies that didn't fall, bones back at the surface,
things that grow in the small worlds of our pitlands,
but not enough history, not an encyclopaedia entry.

East Midlands Designer Outlet, Summer Term 2010[*]

The main industry… was historically coal mining but after the mines closed…
it changed to light industry, warehousing, retailing, and the service sector.
— *Wikipedia entry for Alfreton: Economy*

There's a crack in the kitchen floor of *Subway*, the Brand
Auditor is not happy but what can the Assistant Manager say.
It's sinking. Everything around here is sinking. It's not the way
we're built, it's what we're built on. It's hollow. Tipping

in all the world's bread, lettuce, pre-sliced salami and chicken
won't fix it and besides, Thursdays are for late night shopping
and year elevens are gathering in the food court for something
to do. Familiar cliques from school around *Burger King* fries,

dieting girls at *Spud-u-Like*. They take home nothing.
What they don't know, because nobody told them, is Edwin
was only three older than them, when there was a pit head
here before a tragedy. The girl picks at crushed potatoes

with fancy ham and rocket, has a boyfriend that she's kept secret.
He is the same age as Edwin was when something exploded.
He never came up. The girl was here when she was small
and someone cut a ribbon on opening day. She knows sadness

is in the ground of so many places, but not here.
She doesn't know these names.

[*] Edwin Samuel Hill (19) was one of seven men killed in the South Normanton
Colliery explosion on the 15th of February 1937. East Midlands Designer Outlet
opened in 1998 on the site and a plaque commemorating the men who died was
installed in 2022.

James Dean Bradfield is in my way in *Tescos*

I am trying to buy peppers – we chargrill them
with aubergine, then bake with D.O.P. feta
the nice tomatoes, we steal from a shelf
in the shared kitchen and the aspirational spice mix
I brought back from two repeated weeks somewhere.

We have olive bread and red wine, live our student
depiction of decadence. But today, James Dean Bradfield
is in my way in *Tescos*. His trolley is preventing me
from peppers, while he looks at some vegetable
I don't remember. I want to say 'excuse me'

but cannot swallow all the sentences that would
follow such a statement. So I linger,
looking at avocados, despite my budgetary
distance from their smooth luxury. I keep all of it silent.
Shoppers continue with their onions.

I am huge and conscious in this new world
where both of us perform the business of shopping.
Later, I see him again, bending at the knee to examine
spice shelves, full of *Schwartz* approximate flavours
from the places I easily know that he has been.

GRWM For a Looming Personal Crisis*

This Saturday I am fixing my whole life
by watching a woman's trip food shopping,
uploaded to *YouTube*. I am absorbing order
from her nutrients, I know she will soak
those pulses, has firm plans for brown rice.
If I can do this too, I will achieve her level
of beautiful and I have come to realise,
what will fix my life is being beautiful.
We mustn't say it, she would never say it,
with her white teeth and high cheekbones,
her cream blouse and her husky voice,
but we both know it. When I was depressed
I watched old episodes of *Live Well for Less*,
but those people were ordinary, eating
canned soup, low fat yogurt, *Warburton*'s bread.

The woman has been listening to audiobooks
on habit forming and intentional living.
This is what I must do, instead of replaying
the same records from when I was seventeen.
The problem in my life is my own inaction
and I should fix all this by next Saturday,
which will be bright, crisp and freezing.
My airy home will be a soft-lit haven
of wood-wick soy candles in seasonal scents.
My stomach will have settled, ready
for the brunch aesthetic of poached eggs,
I'll plan recipes to finish my age-old nutmegs.
I will be just who I am by next weekend –
alert at 5AM and bending to make my bed,
billowing clean sheets that fall perfectly.

* GRWM is an acronym used by Youtubers which stands for 'Get Ready With
Me'. The term is used in video titles for example 'GRWM for a day at the
beach' and will generally feature an individual speaking to the camera while
they complete a skincare routine and put on make-up to prepare for the day.

I Assume This is Happening to Everyone

Cartoon Debbie in The Wild Thornberrys, wealth of blonde curls all grunge

and beautiful.

I instruct myself to fancy Jack Ryder in *EastEnders*. Later Sonia will betray me

by becoming a lesbian.

Christina releases 'Dirrty'. She dances in chaps and sweats until her clothes come off.

'It's about being young.'

They repeal Section 28. In form time I say something I'm ashamed of.

Halle Berry is Catwoman.

I consider my pink t-shirt to hang out with a girl. I wonder why I am

worrying.

In Chicago Catherine Zeta Jones does 'All That Jazz', then again, and again.

I ask myself if I fancy her and I point out that I don't. You can think anything.

Rose Tyler in her fresh face and thick black eyeliner.

I know that I am not gay. I remind myself of why.

Keira Knightly stands in a man's shirt in Pirates 3, bare legs over floorboard.

I am logical. Words have their definitions. I believe so much in boxes.

Effy from Skins wears unbelievable fishnets at the start of the second phase.

Nobody comes to tell me this is all completely ordinary.

Before the Words for This

After Carolina Klüft, heptathlete

I was small and my memories are clouded
but to my mind you were grace and domination.

Leading from the front –
why wouldn't you. Launching yourself

into what seemed like the stratosphere.
Blonde shining in every moment,

drawn again and again to the limelight.
Your allure measured in sevens,

the promise of gold, gold, gold on your young neck,
the bold muscularity of your body.

I had not understood my joy in you
until this moment of rediscovery,

not as beautiful as I remember, but captivating,
when you run, when you jump, when you throw.

For the Drag Queen Who Lives in My Building

It's obvious that I have noticed you – all the extremes
of your body, in the smoking shelter you make from
our shared doorway, but I don't talk to anyone. Shame
fills my mouth like the padding around a pulled tooth.
When I see you, I smile. Then smile again. I am still
the same stranger to you, but I know dressing-gown
or full drag, that you are a total body of commitment.
I see the coffee jar you leave for your fag ends,
hiding my face on the way to communal bins.
When I imagine being enough of something,
I imagine you. Proud. Hailing yourself a taxi.
Knowing the meaning of the word.

Whisper It

What was the name of that game we played,
pooling our answers on the playground
to questions like 'favourite flavour crisps?'
or 'boy you want to kiss?'

But it was a girl, the first time
I felt what I learnt is a pull
to pressed lips. I waited
with boys for something different.
They don't use the word on television –
don't even whisper it.

She works at a shop in my hometown, where the truth
of myself is still looming and massive, at the spot
where I found a delayed first kiss –
where I came late to what this feeling is.

You know I asked my mum once, 'am I frigid?'

The small girls answer, 'prawn cocktail, Jordan'
'salt and vinegar, Michael' and I don't know
that I am enough of anything, floundering,
'pickled onion *Monster Munch*,'
I am still whispering it.

She's Lost Control

You are never far from a drunk man in a Joy Division t-shirt.
The old men gather around the cribbage board
and from between them he emerges. He does not know
that *The Atrocity Exhibition* is a novel by Ballard
or recognise the pattern of a pulsar. The same way you do not
know the meanings of flowers, or Latin, the names of famous
painters, or anything. You know this because you ask him
at every occasion. You are raw acne conscious of your
matching attire. You make veiled reference to Peter Hook,
giving yourself conspicuous permission. On occasion
you have wanted to fuck the drunk man in a Joy Division t-shirt
because you were young, stupid, vulnerable or he was hot.
You do not have the necessary compulsion for mistakes.
Having never existed when Joy Division existed, you are
uncomfortable in your presentation of culture. Nervous.
Wherever you go, you are testing the universe of knowledge
around you, gathering up physics and post-punk drumming
without the confidence required to push back what's coming.

What They Meant When They Said 'Beatlemania'

Was that if you looked at the women you might assume an atrocity
was happening, and that you might have made the same case for sex.
That having released themselves into the concept of excitement,
half the population could now cast about for vessels to conduct
their screams. That they were settling on these Liverpudlians in suits.
That it was as much, or more, about women than it was about the men.

What they meant was, all of them were in floods of unexpected tears,
joy but also an end point, how they knew that something had finished.
When we pause those girls on that shudder film, those actual reels
of holdable cellulose, acetate – they look like they are in agony.

What it is to be a woman. We have invented enough that everything
either is or was by this point. Still the women are screaming
while men dance, with nothing of interest in their lack of hysteria.
They meant that we should love those women, building this world
permitting us pleasure, forming their mouths into so many circles,
changing the shape of our future and giving themselves a scream.

Small Town Celebrities

Sharon in the supermarket has been there forever;
John the Can with his foot on the brick wall; the lollipop man
(only in his coat); seat left for the man who died in the nice pub;
this week's pedlar of knock off fags; the black family;
the woman who shopped the paedophile teacher;
the overly zealous Christian youth club leader;
the could-have-been professional footballer, limping
in the winter with his phantom knee complaint;
that couple having their obvious affair; the solitary nun;
the lad from school selling speed in the rough pub
the other, with his arm blown off in our year group's war.
Once upon a time the milkman; postman; paedophile teacher;
and that poor girl in long socks, whose dad took the back
of his head off with that inexplicably achieved gun.

'Bindi'

At the beginning of Brownies in the bowls hall,
I sit opposite Charlotte, in the misshapen circle
of small white girls with culottes and crossed legs.
She has pressed a diamante sticker into the centre
of her forehead. As we pass the news around, she calls it
a bindi. The real ones, she says, are pressed in with a pin.
She is two years older. I have no reason not to believe her.

In my bedroom is a Minnie Mouse pin badge with
a rubber butterfly back. Sometimes I press it to the soft
skin inside my nose, jealous of boys who duck out of lessons,
blood dripping on their wobbling teeth. People do these things.
That night, instead, I put it flush to the flat bone above my nose,
mark out a monobrow from this Western memorabilia, marvel
at the might of these women I've been taught to fear.

The Badger is the Largest Predator Currently Active in Britain

We are at *Thorpe Park*, queueing amongst the plastic
rocks and booths selling frozen drinks to children
already sugar-drunk at the thought of it.

Everything around us is intentional, until you ask:
'Don't you have wolves and bears in the forest?'
Later, I will look up your hometown on social media.

Currently I know nothing of the geography of Romania –
where the teeth and claws of fairy tales can still penetrate.
You are disappointed with our small wilderness,

our mechanical thrills. Maybe I will send you an
e-petition on the reintroduction of the Eurasian Lynx.
The shoes of roller-coaster goers show their soles

to the clear sky above us, and we talk about the last wolf
to have been killed in Britain. I see you reach across
your scope of languages, hoping to do justice

to the huge forgotten moment of our violence,
when that last weapon slipped its familiar way in.
The queue moves up. Everything around us is intentional.

D to Punch

You laugh when I claim to know Thebes as well as you.
You remind me of my habit of confusing Greek and Roman gods,
who share the same old chiselled faces.
What you don't know is the summer of 1998,
when I wasted hours on the *Hercules Action Game*.

I haven't learnt your Latin pronunciation – it's true.
But have you battled harpies with a pixellated sword
and collected loose change in the grey city of level four?
The Z key puts a blade in the stomach of a flasher –
show me a woman with space to know more.

Curby

When I look at streets now, I think it would be easy,
slipping into the spaces between parked cars,
agreeing our day's rules and getting to the stuff of it:
the curve of the ball, the strike, the force enough
to bring the thing back – but we all know differently.

The first time we played curby – standing opposite
your house and the Abernethy's we had that orange-
blue basketball and I imagined this was the road
you were not allowed to cross, when you ran away
with your bag of tinned-food and a can-opener

but it wasn't. Time moved us onto the estate that tracked
the A38, by one of those clusters of garages filled
with broken chairs and Christmas lights for rooftops.
We have become used to all this throwing. You shout
'car' when I am standing in the road for the first time.

We fall back as if we are criminals – keep going onto
different roads, and suddenly the distance is months.
We give up on trying, spend too much time going forward,
forward, to imagine the same place would be there
if I picked up your ball and came back.

The Rules of Knuckles

While we remain a cash carrying society, children play this across the nation.
They swap their strategies in secret, the architects of their cruelty unclear.

To play knuckles you must:
- find an unsupervised area of lesson time, a music practice room will usually
  suffice
- place the proximal phalanges of your least favoured hand on the surface
- brace yourself

Players should not confuse the shock of knuckles with the control of a razor
        blade –
that is the unattractive face of pain, and it will earn them no supporters.

To play knuckles you must:
- keep the playing area free of your local word for grasses
- bring a pound coin from your own purse or pocket
- aim with truth, without sympathy

Dedicated opponents may choose to sharpen their instrument with
        equipment
banned from the pencil case. Honour dictates this is disclosed at the outset.

To play knuckles you must:
- blot your fresh blood on poly-blend trousers
- swallow your shame and cover your pride
- know a bad thing when you need it

Hometown Rich

Your dad's a small business owner, five employees
who hate him and a bowtie for the golf club celebration dinner.
Family accountant with a white-collar-prison-documentary aura.
You've got a *Golddigga* puffer jacket and a deep pile carpet
in your home cinema. Money in your mouth like an accident.

Not my nervous hometown posh, Bulgarian ski trips and lunchbox
taramasalata. Car seat too late, stumbling on my urge to say 'mummy'
when the other kids are past it. I'm obvious, like Conrad, the way
he says bastard with an extra 'r' in t, as if years from now, someone
won't hand me champagne in a pint glass I'll mistake for cider.

A Social History of Coffee-To-Go

At first there are leisure centre dispensers: drop-down small plastic,
next to soup, *Bovril*, instant hot chocolate. What mums drink,
while you spin the dial for gobstoppers, browse vending machines.
You are a long way from *Starbucks* with this chlorine smell,
inexplicable council carpet. No one here has said macchiato and meant it.

Then you start to see thin women who must come from the city.
They carry their cardboard cups with American logos: scrawled barista
bastardisations of their rich, unusual names – their promise
of remarkable lovers; their several-months-of-salary handbags.
These emergent green mermaids stranded on Arabica dry land.

One afternoon you are suddenly in A level history, deciding
on subsidised cappuccino, because you've heard of these people
pepped up by caffeine and you are listening to an explanation
of deindustrialisation as if you need it. Exhausting. You are making it work,
like ambient *Carling* at an unsupervised party. Things are easier after.

Time passes and you pile up lids, stamp cards, milk-froth
and double-shot preferences that complicate minimum wage.
Big names move to your small towns. Old women who boiled
their *Nes-caf* in old pans stop saying 'frothy coffee'. They have learnt
to form their rigid mouths around soft, hot, Italian sounds.

Eventually, on a wet-floor clear-sky morning, you have moved
to the shadow of a museum in time for an off-the-shelf autumn.
There's a fresh painted chalet, bamboo or rice husk reusable cup.
Here is a wide-angle moment, opening credits of some such.
Coffee hot in cold air, sometimes, taste it, life's almost good.

Branch Number

The general manager of this *Wetherspoons* has been promoted
beyond his skillset. The boy he hated at primary school, is a man now,
arguing about licensing. He is buying a second pint of cider,
while he sits for lunch with his son who is seven. A toddler is crushing
peas into the pattern of the carpet. Mayonnaise packets are massing
at the condiment station and boxes of frozen British Beef Lasagna
are waiting in the walk-in. Weekends are consistently repeating
and I am lost on the way to the ladies, where someone has thrown up
Marketing's new beverage in an impossible shade of pink. A fruit
machine rattles with sounds unlikely to be victory. Business meeting
and hangover breakfast. The mums arrive after swimming, chlorine hair,
catch-up, *J20s* and paninis. These days are on draught, new locations coming.

You Were at School with the Boy from Narnia

Not Edmund, who filled us with false promises
of Turkish Delight and fantasies of Tilda Swinton.
But the other one, Peter, with all the appropriate
values for a boy named *Son of Adam.*

His uprightness was irrelevant to me, but typically
you loved him. You tell me the girls from grammar school
would follow him – excited by whatever part
of being near to James McAvoy still lingered.

I wonder, what became of the boy who should
have been that year's upper sixth attraction.
If things were measured by their normal rankings,
without a film star in your corner of the Cotswolds:

the footballer, the good hair, the one who everyone swears
is 'going out with a model actually'. I need to know
if he can claw back his moment, if he knows he lost
what was promised, the hearts that didn't flutter at his name.

Is he reaching out for a stolen spring?
Eventually, is his thaw coming?

Feather Boy

Or the kid from *Love Actually* – as the world calls you.
Suddenly, I notice you have punctured your soft
earlobe with a delicate ring and gotten big-eyed
beautiful. Life happens – but it's a strange thing
when the children of public consciousness grow up
hot. Troubling. But then we can't tell kids this is what
time is. The way you slip out of the fixed frame
of reference, feet unexpectedly achieving
adult sizes, becoming a shape of the past.

Avril Lavigne Explains Punk to an Uninterested Journalist (2002)

Jesus Christ how they hate her for it.
How a girl would dare to be seventeen
and be asked questions, and give them
answers. The whole world is screaming
to mock her, but regardless she is playing
guitar all around the unforgivable west
and you might say badly, because you
are a bastard, and surely that is the point
of all of this. You watch this decade-
and-the-rest-old viral video from the toilet
having decided that it is not punk rock
to get enough fiber in your diet. She says
it is more punk to tell people you aren't punk
and she's more right than you've ever been.
She's growing up just a rock chick.
She likes to yell and get her anger out.

'Second Adolescence'

I told you in passing one evening but you –
having encountered the latest *Charlie's Angels* trailer,
are having your bisexual awakening loudly.

Now that we have come to worship at the altar
of KStew, my *Instagram* suggestions are full
of *Twilight*. Something I know nothing about,
having shunned things important to young women
in my attempt to authentically be a young woman.

When we are late to the truths of ourselves
we still follow that pattern like kids do:
buying their fish net gloves, throwing
off old idols, squeaky clean men
and *Smash Hits*. Discovering, circling
back to discover again.

If you consider time in a non-linear manner,
we were bound to overcome this lie together –
eventually one of us will have asked.

Use Hard Shoulder in Emergencies

On long drives, you notice the nowhere dystopia
of motorways – smashed lightbulb on the side
of a travelling fairground ride. Digital signage
screaming: 'Don't drive tired', 'Don't drink and drive.'
Rattling over fatal collision sites and the unseen
scattering of unremarkable hometowns. Wildflowers
bursting brave in unkempt verges. And the dead things
and the dead things and the scraping and scooping
of the dead things. Time-marked asphalt, scattered
with rubber blown from burst tyres. Shh-thwack
of rain on the window screen as you pass under a B-road
bridge. The service station slip road that greets you
in anonymity, with its enormous coffee cup and limp
chips. Broken wing-mirror glistening in sinking
sunlight, trees fruiting with plastic, hurtling into night.

West

It's best to re-enter Wales at dusk. Avoid The Bridge.
Dive from the Midlands into Monmouth and at the *croeso* –
wind down your window, play 'Motorcycle Emptiness'
to the famous air. Drive fast on the green roads,
they have little need for motorways just there.
Now gather what the English call consonants.
Cast off these new Latin vowels. Steady yourself.
If you must take the M4 into Cardiff, go slow.
Mention those red trees that smother the hillsides
to the empty passenger seat or better yet, head west,
worrying the shape of the country until you find the sea.
Rain will fall in the mountains and meet you there by morning.

Proceeded to Drink Several Pints of *Brains*

I know I don't sound Cardiff, still
holding the taste of another accent,
but there are parts of this city that keep
my heart in their stone hands.

Worst mistake and very best beginnings.

I remember the first time I heard *Brains*.
That strange word for a drink on the mouth
of a Welshman. I remember the Welshman.

Then the mornings, filled with those hops,
spreading their story on the new day's air.
All gone now. Consistently different city,
how quickly these old things clear.

Michael Sheen Keeps Parking His Car at My Office

When BAFTA award winner Michael Sheen is due to park his car at my office,
people loiter in bay windows, hoping for a barbecue story about the time they saw him –
like when Camilla Parker-Bowles visited across the way – but so much Welsher.

Workflow is diminished, as we wait for the car I will not describe. No one admits
to what is happening. Nobody says *celebrity*. I stay at my desk like with Camilla.
This has become a performance. Even the traffic lights interfere with the city –

shifting pace to give the unsuspecting a glimpse of him. There would be no answer,
if I were to ask why we do this. Some days or hours later, Sheen collects his car
from my office. The city regroups, regathers. The window is open. I say something

loud and hilarious from my ergonomic desk chair. This demonstrates that
I too am an artist. Nothing happens. Minutes later, the car I won't describe
has vanished. Look, this happened twice and here I am, telling you all about it.

Dartington Crystal Factory and Visitor Centre, October 2022

Sign two tells me: 'Glass is allowed to cool
to a working temperature of 1100°C'.
As if such things are ordinary.

Glass craftsmen, one woman, roll, flatten
and blow their violent globs of molten
orange yellow, around tourists who are more
or less interested.

Here are two places at once.

One with phrases like 'cracking off the moil'.
One for people taking themselves out
of the habit of things, loitering in gift shops
and car parks. Nowhere has statis like a tourist
attraction, sliced ice pressed in a guidebook.

There is life happening and there is nothing,
but this is a workplace, so the radio is blasting
inaccuracies, on the link between thunder and rain.

A man expands a void inside a fast-cooling casing.
The exhibition boards explain he has been here longer
than the safety railings. He is fond of golf and sailing.

He blows glass.

Everything that has been here
is moments away from shattering.

Tell Me Again About Your Visa Application

Look, I just don't care about this travelling.
Not that I'm uninterested in the Terracotta Army –
just that I was a sad child, busy being sad
on the balconies of Euro package holidays.

I was sent to bed while someone's leathery dad
sang 'Mustang Sally' at poolside karaoke.
Once in a post-Soviet après bar, an instructor
showed me the honest metal of his gun.

I am uninterested in your travelling without
a prior understanding of your fixed income
and your *Hilton Honours* membership status.
I find so many people cannot distinguish

between a nice view and just being high up.
'Fucking just get on with something,' I want
to say, because I have to live the way I live,
embarrassed of this body, in a new or old place.

In the Philippines I Hear They Sell Spaghetti

How will you come to untangle the various *McDonald's*™
of your life. Which one for the best friends' seventh birthday,
first strawberry milkshake, the after dentist treat? Which one
with the girl from swimming lessons, crying in the strip-lit window?
Which one where you sat in a sad booth, while your fellow teenagers
fucked in the accessible toilet? What does Oxford look like?
French *McDonald's*™ selling beer, last Euros on *McLattee*™
in an airport location. Drive-thru. Everything significant I remember,
tastes of pre-sliced gherkin. I shuffle the bright *Happy Meal*™ toys
of my memory, scars of hot apple pie, freshly invented *McFlurry*™.
Best play area, drunk student demanding an NUS card cheeseburger.
Prefab popping up, when you turn your back on a small town
destination. *McNuggets*™ are repeatable, boot shaped chicken
product, dropped again and again on an indistinct lino floor.

The Cheeseburger Love Song

At the window is a woman you have loved despite your diet,
gorged on the look of her with the guiltiest parts of hunger.
Her deft hands dance on the wax wrap paper, forearms
flecked with a hundred spitting oil scars. The fast-food tattoo.
She is always here, and you suppose she remembers you,
from her unkissed acne years and all the warm paper bags between.
You, who would surrender your torso to the drive-thru window,
to take her by the over-washed polo-shirt collar and to have her.
Her lips would have the cherry pink taste of market stall gloss,
her mouth drenched in free fills of fountain cola. The thing is,
she has seen you, all of your faces in those repeated flash cars.
She could make you in a minute. Plunge your heart and her hand
into the deep fat, feel nothing. You are ruined, crisp and bubbling.

In The Parallel Universe of Our Affair

We arrange our conference hotels for
the convenience of each other's bodies
and gloriously individual beds. In ten
years we have shared neither mirror
nor sink. We do not worry if people see us.
The south east delegation is all aware.
I spill bad coffee in break-out sessions –
a new excuse for that sheer blouse
in the afternoon. I don't think of you
when you're out of my vision. I'm confident
at the cinemas and supermarkets of home.
I have made hazy moral peace with this.
I don't know if I fancy you anymore.
The practice of you thrills me, like
an occasional lottery ticket. I admit
your cock continues to be worth it.
There's me bleeding through from the universe,
where we are yet to kiss. I know you are
an excellent kisser. You take diligent notes
on delegate lists. Drudgery and the promise
of life as we live it – name badge
and legal pad routine of this, this, this.

LinkedIn Recruiter Meets Candidates for Surrealism

I met a candidate today and although he was seven minutes late,
I still shook his hand, and it transformed into a paint brush,
and when he ran his bristles over the beige wall he left behind
the opening scene from *Trainspotting*. I stepped into the image
and Ewan MacGregor stopped running to tell me that when he interviews
drug dealers he pours two glasses of water but leaves them untouched
on the table. His pale fist punched me in my baffled face. I fell out
of the painting of a poster, into a new blank room with a panel
of C suite members gathered around an artificial pot plant, watering it
with *Fanta Fruit Twist* and muttering about the quarterly outputs.
I fled out of the window and scaled down the side of the building
with the new claws I'd made from demonstrating efficiency savings.
I knew that if I just rescued a drowning dog from a cold canal
I would encounter its master in my second stage interview
and become the punchline of a cautionary tale. I did not apologise.
My smartphone transformed into an *Uno Extreme* device and spewed
business cards down the embarrassed front of my chinos. I picked up four
and they were covered in quotes from Steven Bartlett. I put them
in my pocket and shook my own hand. I was seven minutes late
and turning into a paint brush. Comment below if you agree.

We Would Like You to Become Your Own Boss

Everybody here knows that when statutory maternity pay ends,
you cannot cover the cost of your low paying job. So hollow
out your social spaces and fill them with our lipsticks.

We applaud your rejection of the wage labour economy.

Here is a motivational image we suggest you share on *Facebook*,
where we have rearranged words like 'entrepreneur', 'six-figure,'
and 'empower.' Please understand that when you break the seal
of the starter kit, your products become used and unreturnable.

A free sample selection of our mushroom coffee
alternatives is £7.95 for shipping.

The key to sales is unshakeable confidence in your product.
We suspect that you may struggle to produce this
and have provided substitute copy, which we doubt
anyone will recognise as our voice in your soft mouth.

Today while you are being your own boss, we would like
you to host a party selling sex toys to women from school,
who remember you as a teenager, spreading whispered information
about the taste of a penis behind temporary classrooms.
Package their orders discreetly, hope you remember their address.

Keep it going.

Please do not seek legal representation.

Considering the Fertility Window

I have been swallowing years since seventeen,
when my first friend told me there were cells splitting
just south of her stomach. Somewhere the 'I'm pregnant'
answer slips to 'congratulations' from 'fuck'.

Now the babies cover my timeline, from accidents
and marriages, plans, prayers and progressively talked
about test tubes. There are babies, babies, babies,
but also toddlers, tricycles, front teeth, school uniforms

and more and more candles crowding onto cakes
from ages I remember. The two MAs marriage
is posting an ultrasound, the lesbians adopting
from Vietnam. Those cells from seventeen

are a personality, walking through rain in a big blazer,
classic year seven November. I have time.
I am telling myself to make a decision
but that truth is shrinking. I've grown up so fast.

The Year of the Fish Pedicure

Remember them? Out on display in the shopping centre,
taking up the *Calendar Club* Christmas spot, in the early years
of embarrassing mums buying twelve gloss pages of Channing Tatum.

Looking out on a new *Primark* and back then, *BHS* and *Debenhams*.
Cosmopolitan. 'This is something that would happen on 'Sex In The City,'
says a woman, who has never seen an episode. Her tired red-nail feet
rest in a clear dish bowl, that shows off these hard-working
aquatic carnivores. Local evolution had no time for this, but now,
international mail order, Red Garra, shoals of tiny lost nibble fish.

If we followed the fish pedicure money, if we scaled down
drains, and cheap spa alleyways, where did these fish industries
come from? The women? We remember it was women. We notice
these worlds of only women. Where did they go? What traffic
have we emptied into our water pipes? What's the next thing
after bubble tea and waxed occasional truckles of cheese?
Quick turnover business. The kids these days already have feet
that were never gnawed on by something without options.
Something else is out there hungry for the flesh of ourselves.

You Wouldn't Download the Exquisite Pleasures of the Flesh

For cruel fear of not experiencing them properly –
the dot, bit, pixelation of their promise rendering
them dual-screen distracting and un-focusable.

You wouldn't risk the dissatisfaction of inappropriate
subtitling on the moment of your heart's desire.
You wouldn't settle for a pirate copy of ecstasy,

the shadow of a small-bladdered woman passing
in front of everything you had ever wished for.
You would sit silent on Sunday afternoons

under the crush of ideological inertia. You would wait
for the best thing rather than anything. Cry out
to be good in the darkness, desperate to be moral
in the unacceptable face of your ongoing living.

I'm Not As Much of a Runner As I Claim to Be

The woman who visits the park opposite,
has taken up a half translated Swedish habit,
she calls it 'plogging', but that's a word
I would rather keep unsaid.

She runs, picks up detritus, as if she has forgotten
that nobody in the real world comes
within half a mile of the word *detritus.*

Sometimes she brings a carrier bag – from the carrier
bag of carrier bags in her kitchen. At others,
she is faster but still lunges for the blue
plastic chip fork by the bins.

Her hamstrings move in the right ways.

She is in the supermarket in her active-wear.
Still a runner while perfectly still –
choosing tomatoes.

The strength in her legs makes me wonder –
why I can't help but hate the best of us.

I have practiced calling him Peter

For 'Pete' Doherty

In the noughties, our pavements were littered with your dropped Rs,
cast from the mouths of the public, the typesetters of tabloids,
the music business. Occasionally, if you knew how to watch,
a sad girl would stop to pick one up. A carrier, a confidante, misattributed
Libertine – small, safe, still sheltered from the worst things.

Sometimes, I am still that sad girl. I have practiced enough of my life
that I am in the habit of calling him Peter. Every time it is a beacon
of love and mockery. Love I was taught to carry like shame,
because everything wrong with him is catching.

My friends were yet to give up on pop punk.
I had decided to say things about Rimbaud
and Baudelaire, and so, I practiced calling him Peter.
I practiced radical acceptance at a bruised arm's length.
I imagined letters to Wormwood, Pentonville.

Now targeted ads ask me to buy tickets for that part
of my past but I haven't and maybe I won't.
I am showing myself how different my life is
to the one that pavement-picking girl imagined.
I am doing these things although I don't know how,

but me and her love our idea of him
and I carry that now for both of us,
somebody's father,
somebody's brother,
somebody's son,
somebody.

The Water Cycle

Occasionally, the weather lifts to let layers
of time shift. Then you walk into the night
and find water, dark and quiet, in this place

of all teenagers wishing for the huge sound
of an escaping sea. The chance of an unseen
horizon and the wash wash warm idea

of the future. All these realities stack up
on each other. There is no frame for emotions
when they are happening altogether.

On some sea front, a girl is picking souvenir
threads for the braid she is growing, cutting,
keeping. She is drunk in a musician's basement.

She is getting older, married, filing her taxes, presenting
the news. She is still on every bench in the dark park –
dreaming the promising sounds of any sea.

Intermittent Phone Call

My grandmother talks about her mortality, her frozen
meals, what's happening in the garden, how she reads
a book a day, gathers bargains from the charity shop
to plough through and make my uncle give back.

She has been clearing her house for more years
than I can remember. We have given up on telling her
to stop. Still when I visit, there is a *Complete Works
of Shakespeare* which as far as I know it, has never moved

from the glass fronted cabinet. She has stopped having a tree
at Christmas, but decorates the house with meant-for-parcel
ribbons. She is smaller now than she ever was. There is a hut
for her mobility scooter. She has begun to shun invitations,

my father and cousins fish them from her bin.
If I were to get married it is unlikely she would attend.
I have eaten more cheese triangles in her house
than could have been good for me. The long dead dog
licked toffee yogurt dregs from our Saturday afternoon pots.

It is hard to imagine it will not always be.
Her house will give way to someone else.
She warns us but we ignore her because she is old
and repeats and repeats herself.

Punks Consider the Dylan Thomas Theatre

On my eighteenth birthday, I saw John Cooper Clarke in Derby.
Now that is irrelevant and despite turning thirty, I wear
a leather zip-up dress and Doc Martens while Gillian Clarke

reads poetry in Swansea. She mentions war, the wine is terrible.
She talks of chaos; the bar is only cash. She covers climate change,
ice is falling massive from mountains. I have driven here.

I drive back remembering Vivienne Westwood is recently dead.
It's a wound I don't know how to mention. The world gives us
so few old women. It doesn't like their thin skin. It knows memories

they were forced to make. It is nervous at the shock of their reality.
My knuckleduster ring twitches. The teeth are loose in my head.
Sometimes I dream of them crumbling. I want to shout at nothing
in particular. Eventually none of us will wake up one morning.

Before David Bowie Died

I would think about it coming sometimes –
that macabre statistical promise
in my small imagining of the universe.

How on that day, I'd wear a lightning bolt
on a shirt I have dreamt of but never found.
How in my interesting places
people would recognise the loss in me.

At some point, I believed, I would have laid
my eyes on his – predicting myself such futures.

My expectations of the German Foreign Office were non-existent.

On whatever sides of our walls we land on,
we can breathe something out: something in.

I pictured myself as older than I turned out
to be, and when it happened the day
was colder than I had come to expect.
There was no rain to shine on the tiles
of the townhouse I didn't own
and I am sorry to report,

that I didn't look at the world
from an unexplored distance,
or put out new hands
in search of the wonderful.

'The Grease Megamix' Closes a Party

For a while the DJ tries to be current, but then 'Tiger Feet'
into 'Come On Eileen', then the 'YMCA' and Pulp.
I love Pulp. At this point I am 72% Britpop and I know

that I am a product of this place. Queueing at the buffet,
for half cobs of egg mayonnaise; silver-skin onions,
cheese, pineapple; quiche stacked on white paper plates.

The kids and the women have taken their shoes off
and white socks skid on the chipped varnish floor,
danger that's so much slower than I remember.

There's something about the shape of this hall,
the heat never finds its way in. There's been a chill
on every red wine ever served here and memories

gather in the high roof amongst the home-pumped
helium balloons. We know we'll all be here again.
The paint has worn off the sign but we can read it.

I sat for years on the car-park wall and watched
for the future, but after the split lines of girls and guys
sang their drunken high notes, we go to our same homes –

safe on wide streets without traffic, all those summer nights.

Acknowledgments

My enormous thanks to my friend and editor Rhian Edwards who has been my cheerleader from almost the moment she met me. Huge thanks as well to the excellent Zoë Brigley, and the wider Seren team including Amy Wack and the late Mick Felton.

'The Day of the Flying Ants', 'Bindi', and 'The Cheeseburger Love Song', appeared in my 2019 smith|doorstop pamphlet *The Day of the Flying Ants*. Thanks and apologies to Peter Sansom who edited that pamphlet and didn't receive my thanks at the time.

'Branch Number' was first published in *bath magg*, 'Hometown Rich', 'When My Father Dies' and 'A Speculative Script for Motherhood' were first published in *Poetry Wales*. 'Before the Words for This' and 'I Am Not As Much of a Runner as I Claim to Be' were first published in *The North*. 'The Grease Megamix Closes a Party' was first published in *The Waxed Lemon*. 'Installing A Terrarium in the Town Square', 'Love Song to a Poster Boy' and 'Before David Bowie Died' were first published in *Confluences*. 'East Midlands Designer Outlet...' was first published in *Derwent Press*. 'Whisper It' was first published in *Shooter*. 'For the Drag Queen Who Lives in My Building' was first published in the Broken Spine anthology *Reels*. 'The Badger is the Largest Predator...' was first published in the Broken Sleep anthology *Footprints*.

Thanks to the wonderful women of Answers on a Postcard: Rhian Edwards (again), Julie Griffiths, Tracey Rhys, Susie Wild, Marcelle Newbold, Amanda Rackstraw, and Emily Blewitt – who have workshopped so many poems with me over tea, wine, hummus, artfully arranged scotch eggs, and giant prawn cocktail Wotsits.

Thanks to Dan, HN&D. Thanks to the family and friends who have supported my long-term poetic strangeness – special thanks to B. Mure for telling me it was OK to want to do things when we were both 16.

And as for all the things that would usually follow such a statement: this book wouldn't exist without Nicky, Richey, James, and Sean. God Save the Manics.

The Author

Emily Cotterill is a Cardiff based poet originally from Alfreton in Derbyshire. Her debut pamphlet *The Day of the Flying Ants* (smith | doorstop, 2019) was selected by Carol Ann Duffy as a part of the Laureate's Choice series. Writing about place, identity and pop-culture, her poetry has appeared in *Poetry Wales, The North, bath magg, The Waxed Lemon* and various other magazines, online journals and anthologies including the 2024 *COAL* anthology commemorating 40 years since the Miners' Strike.